FELIXSTOWE

A Photographic History of Your Town

DAVID TOLLIDAY has lived in the town since 1945 and has a collection of local material gathered over the past 57 years. He is currently the Manager of Landguard Fort on behalf of the Landguard Fort Trust.

FELIXSTOWE

A Photographic History
of Your Town

DAVID TOLLIDAY

WH
S

First published in the United Kingdom in 2002 by
Black Horse Books especially for WHSmith Limited

British Library Cataloguing in Publication Data

Felixstowe
a photographic history of your town
David Tolliday
ISBN 1-904033-76-8

Black Horse Books
Frith's Barn, Teffont,
Salisbury, Wiltshire SP3 5QP
Tel: +44 (0) 1722 716 376
Fax: +44 (0) 1722 716 881

www.francisfrith.co.uk

Printed and bound in Great Britain

Contents

The Making of an Archive

Francis Frith, Victorian founder of the world-famous photographic archive, was a devout Quaker and a highly successful Victorian businessman. By 1860 he was already a multi-millionaire, having established and sold a wholesale grocery business in Liverpool. He had also made a series of pioneering photographic journeys to the Nile region. The images he returned with were the talk of London. An eminent modern historian has likened their impact on the population of the time to that on our own generation of the first photographs taken on the surface of the moon.

Francis Frith 1822-1898

Frith had a passion for landscape, and was as equally inspired by the countryside of Britain as he was by the desert regions of the Nile. He resolved to set out on a new career and to use his skills with a camera. He established a business in Reigate as a specialist publisher of topographical photographs.

Frith lived in an era of immense and sometimes violent change. For the poor in the early part of Victoria's reign work was a drudge and the hours long, and ordinary people had precious little free time. Most had not travelled far beyond the boundaries of their own town or village. Mass tourism was in its infancy during the 1860s, but during the next decade the railway network and the establishment of Bank Holidays and half-Saturdays gradually made it possible for the working man and his family to enjoy holidays and to see a little more of the world. With characteristic business acumen, Francis Frith foresaw that these new tourists would enjoy having souvenirs to commemorate their days out. He began selling photo-souvenirs of seaside resorts and beauty spots, which the Victorian public pasted into treasured family albums.

Frith's aim was to photograph every town and village in Britain. For the next thirty years he travelled the country by train and by pony and trap, producing fine photographs of seaside resorts and beauty spots that were keenly bought by millions of Victorians.

The Rise of Frith & Co

Each photograph was taken with tourism in mind, the small team of Frith photographers concentrating on busy shopping streets, beaches, seafronts, picturesque lanes and villages. They also photographed buildings: the Victorian and Edwardian eras were times of huge building activity, and town halls, libraries, post offices, schools and technical colleges were springing up all over the country. They were invariably celebrated by a proud Victorian public, and photo souvenirs - visual records - published by F Frith & Co were sold in their hundreds of thousands. In addition, many new commercial buildings such as hotels, inns and pubs were photographed, often because their owners specifically commissioned Frith postcards or prints of them for re-sale or for publicity purposes.

In order to gain some understanding of the scale of Frith's business one only has to look at the catalogue issued by Frith & Co in 1886: it runs to some 670 pages. By 1890 Frith had created the greatest specialist photographic publishing company in the world, with over 2,000 stockists! The picture below shows the Frith & Co display board on the wall of the stockist at Ingleton in the Yorkshire Dales. Beautifully constructed with mahogany frame and gilt inserts, it displayed a dozen scenes.

Postcard Bonanza

The ever-popular holiday postcard we know today took many years to appear, and F Frith & Co was in the vanguard of its development. Postcards became a hugely popular means of communication and sold in their millions. Frith's company took full advantage of this boom and soon became the major publisher of photographic view postcards.

Francis Frith died in 1898 at his villa in Cannes, his great project still growing. His sons Eustace and Cyril continued their father's monumental task, expanding the number of views offered to the public and recording more and more places in Britain, as the coasts and countryside were opened up to mass travel. The archive Frith created continued in business for another seventy years. By 1970 it contained over a third of a million pictures of 7,000 cities, towns and villages. The massive photographic record Frith has left to us stands as a living monument to a special and very remarkable man.

This book shows your town as it was photographed by this world-famous archive at various periods in its development over the past 150 years. Every photograph was taken for a specific commercial purpose, which explains why the selection may not show every aspect of the town landscape. However, the photographs, compiled from one of the world's most celebrated archives, provide an important and absorbing record of your town.

Introduction

The town of Felixstowe, which lies at the southern end of the Colneis peninsular between the Rivers Orwell and Deben, is fortunate in many ways.

It is fortunate geographically because the two rivers which surround it are two of the very few safe landfalls between the Thames and the Humber, making it a desirable location. It is fortunate meteorologically because although it is on the east coast, it faces south, giving it a pleasing climate. It is fortunate geologically because within less than a mile of the coast it is blessed with a strip of rich agricultural land. It is fortunate militarily because it has always had the benefits of continuous military occupation from the Romans, through Saxon, medieval, Tudor, and Victorian times, up to the 20th-century Army, Navy and Air Force. It is fortunate economically because with all these things in its favour, it can always survive, even if one of these factors declines. The photographs in this book cover the period from the late 19th to the early 21st century; during this time, Felixstowe's agriculture declined, but its role as a seaside resort increased. This role in turn declined, and was replaced by a thriving port, now the largest in the country.

The Gardens and Cliff Hotel 1907 58965

Introduction

The West End

As we travel to Felixstowe along the A14, we are directed to turn right at the dock spur roundabout and follow this very busy main road to the entrances to Felixstowe Docks.

In the last few years, these docks have become the largest container port in the UK, the fourth largest in Europe, which ranks Felixstowe as one of the major seaports of the world. However, it is true to say that the port barely touches the parish of Felixstowe: most of it is in neighbouring Walton, and its northern extremity is in Trimley. How different this is to the landscape caught in our earliest photographs in this collection; in 43233 (above), for instance, note the empty landscape receding into the distance. This view is now dominated by giant cranes and acres of warehousing.

The man who can claim the credit for starting this transformation is George Tomline of Orwell Park, Nacton, which is situated further up the peninsular towards Ipswich. George Tomline held the honorary rank of Colonel in the Lincolnshire Militia, and despite his never having served in the Army, was always referred to as Colonel Tomline. He was born into a very rich family and was educated at Eton, where he was regarded by Sir Robert Peel as one of

The West End

Towards Harwich 1899
43233

A wide view of the West Beach from above the remains of the gun battery below Martello Q. Commercial enterprise is burgeoning with L M Capon's fancy bazaar (left). This is now the site of the leisure centre.

the two most intelligent boys in the school - the other was William Gladstone. Like Gladstone, he moved into politics; he was elected unopposed for the Sudbury constituency as a Tory (Conservative) party MP. He did not remain a Tory for long: although he became the member for Shrewsbury in 1841 (his running mate in the constituency was Benjamin Disraeli), he lost his seat in 1847, and promptly changed his allegiance to the Liberals. He was re-elected for Shrewsbury in 1852, 1857, 1859 and 1865. He stood for election to the Grimsby constituency in 1867, but he lost East Suffolk in the 1874 poll, thus ending 22 years of continuous service in parliament. He bought Orwell Park in 1841, and continued to extend this estate by buying agricultural properties whenever he could. In 1867 he bought the estate of the Duke of Hamilton, together with the lordship of the manor of Walton with Trimley - this included the area now occupied by the port.

In 1875 Tomline started promoting a bill to authorise the construction of a tidal basin, but it was not until 1886 that it was opened for shipping. In the meantime he built and opened a railway between Westerfield (Ipswich) and Felixstowe in 1877. Again, we must be careful

The West End

Above: **Sea Road 1907** 58970

Two of the many horse-drawn cabs plying for fares along Sea Road.

Left: **Behind the Beach 1907** 58975

The large tent (far left) was the forerunner of the Pier Pavilion, which is where the White Coons concert party performed between 1906 and 1909 when a permanent structure was erected. The site for the model yacht pond seems to be under way, though this was not opened until 1910 - so may be what we see is the remains of flooding.

of terminology, as this railway did not run into the actual parish of Felixstowe; Tomline had rivals for the development of Felixstowe, and he may well have avoided the competition with his first railway venture. At the same time, Tomline was making plans to site the town of Felixstowe on this low-lying western area. Although some land was sold for speculative development, and a manor house was built, the venture was not successful, particularly when compared with the expansion of the central cliff-top area that was going on at the same time.

We leave the A14 at Dock Gate Number 2. It is the main street of Tomline's town, known as Walton Avenue, that leads us past Gate 1 and over the railway crossing, with the original wooden Beach Station on the left-hand side (the building is now being used by a printer). The railway is still used for freight traffic from the docks.

By turning right into Langer Road and following the signs to Landguard Point, we arrive at Felixstowe's only Grade I ancient monument, Landguard Fort. Though the present fort's walls date from 1744, these are the fourth walls to be built here at the end of the peninsula where the rivers Orwell and Stour meet the sea. Its great claim to fame is that it repulsed an attempt at invasion by the Dutch in 1667; this was the last opposed landing on English shores. The fort has recently undergone consolidation under English Heritage's patronage. It is leased to the Landguard Fort Trust, a local charity, who man it and open it to the public throughout the year. The Felixstowe Museum is also on this site.

Past the fort and towards the river there is a

The West End

The Old Pier 1907 58985

The West End

We are looking over the Orwell/Stour estuary towards Harwich from the beach near the dock entrance. The pier was the landing point for the steamers from Ipswich, which brought thousands of visitors to the town - it was a popular excursion.

viewing point donated by the Port of Felixstowe, enabling the public to watch the comings and goings of shipping in and out of the river - this is a very popular spot, and must be one of the finest ship-watching platforms in the world. Retracing our route back to the main road, and turning right into Manor Road, we approach Colonel Tomline's manor house. This was originally built as a hotel, and was then used as the first golf club in Felixstowe, before being a private house. Tomline lived there in 1887-88. It has had many uses since, including a school, military accommodation and a social club. It also had a swimming pool to which pupils from the town's schools would walk for lessons; it is a long way from the town centre, and such a trek would, no doubt, be frowned upon by the education authority of today. The pool never reopened after being damaged in the 1953 floods. These floods caused the death of 39 people, all of whom lived in this low-lying western area.

Nearby is another of the town's military relics, the Martello Tower P. These towers were built around the coast to counter the threat of Napoleonic attack, and eight were erected along the Walton/Felixstowe coast line. The N tower is in Ferry Lane, Walton; O is at Landguard; Q stands on South Hill (38677, page 18), and R on the south-east cliff; S is towards

The Docks 1907 58986

By 1907 the development of the dock basin was well established. This picture shows (left to right) Marriages flour mill, the Dock Office, dockside warehouses and the Pier Hotel. The hulk on the beach is the remains of a ship broken up by the Dock Company. In 1909 Queen Victoria's yacht the 'Osborne' was broken up here; many artefacts found their way into the town.

The Model Yacht Pond 1922 72593

Sailing model yachts was a very popular pastime. In the background we can see St John's spire. The White Coons are back at the Pier Pavilion.

Felixstowe ferry, T stands on the golf course, and U at Felixstowe ferry itself. Of these, P, Q, T and U remain today as solid reminders of the past. There are around 750,000 bricks in each tower, all of which were landed from barges onto the Felixstowe shore.

To end our tour of the West End, we must return along the promenade towards the new pier. The next building past Martello P is the Herman de Stern Convalescent Home, built in 1902 for patients transferred from the London Hospital, Whitechapel (51265, page 19). Its medical uses are now over. More recently it has been a community centre for the West End, which incorporated a small theatre, now derelict. The building, together with all the land to the west as far as the old manor house, is now part of a new proposed tourist development for the area.

The next attraction is Mannings amusement park (F16026 and F16041, pages 18 and 19). It dates from 1932, when it was opened by Billy Butlin; it remained until the outbreak of World War II in 1939. After re-opening following the war, it was leased by Charlie Manning and his family - the second generation now operates it. New arcades have now been added on the Sea Road frontage. We pass a line of hotels built before WW1; few are still hotels today - old folks' homes and apartments are today's vogue. Then we arrive at the pier area and the central section of the sea front.

The West End

Above: **Sea Road 1896** 38677

Sea Road has a large expanse of foreshore abutting it. The round building (mid-right) is the Martello Tower Q, one of eight built along the Felixstowe shore line. The newsboy in the foreground has few customers! The nearest building on the left was built as a children's home, the first one in the town.

Right: **The Bay looking East c1955** F16026

A view towards the town from the amusement park, with the Felixstowe and Suffolk Bowls Club in the foreground. Bowls players were much less particular on the clothing worn to play than is the case today. We can see how much shorter the pier is after WW2.

The West End

Above: **The Herman de Stern Convalescent Home 1904** 51265

This is the last of the 19th-century convalescent homes; it was specifically for patients discharged from the London Hospital. Later it became used by the Ipswich Hospital Group, replacing the older Suffolk home.

Above: **The Gardens and the Amusement Park c1955** F16041

This was formerly Butlins, and is now Mannings amusement park with its wooden scenic railway, a prominent landmark for many years.

The Central Sea Front

Children's Rides 1907 58978

The Central Sea Front

The Central Sea Front

Above: **Cliff Gardens 1899** 44510

This area was the first municipal attempt at providing publicly-owned visitor attractions. These gardens were established as 'pleasure grounds' in 1888.

Right: **The Beach 1899** 44516

The Victorians flocked to the seaside in large numbers, as we can see from these views of the Central Beach. What they did not do was sunbathe. There were plenty of people catering for the visitors' needs, as we can appreciate from the traders' huts along the beach.

For convenience, I designate the area below the cliffs between the New Pier and Bath Hill as the central sea front. It is the most-photographed part of Felixstowe in our collection.

The New Pier (58974, page 26) was erected by the Coast Development Corporation between 1903 and 1905. It was over 900 yards long; it needed to reach deep water, thus enabling coastal steamers to call and to land passengers on regular services between London and Great Yarmouth. In time, amusements were added to the landward end, and shelters were provided seaward - these could be reached by an electric tramway.

World War II saw the demise of this splendid landmark. On 30 May 1940 the pier was breached about 300 yards along its length as part of the defences against invasion, and it was further damaged by incendiary bombs on

29 August of the same year. Much debate about reopening the pier took place when peace returned, but economic considerations prevailed: it was decided to demolish the greater part of its length and to rebuild the landward end. Even this was controversial, and a local referendum was held to decide who should do this. The Council lost! Now the reduced pier is closed, and will, no doubt, be demolished, unless some body will fund its restoration.

The leisure centre which now stands immediately landward of the pier is on the site of several earlier buildings; of these, a gun battery below Q Tower, the first St John's church and two pier pavilions are worthy of note. The second pavilion (F16050 and F16032, pages 28 and 29) is a fond memory to many of the now older generation of inhabitants who attended the regular dances held there. It had a fine dance floor, and could accommodate up to

The Central Sea Front

1000 customers; this meant that all the best dance bands in the country included it on their regular circuits. I suppose that through the big band era of the 50s and 60s it also made us local yokels feel that we were not the back of beyond either.

The Town Hall is the next place of note (44514, page 28). This was built in 1892 by the Felixstowe and Walton Local Government Board, which was formed in 1887, and met at Bulls Cliff (54646, page 31) until the Town Hall was built. Before this the village, as it then was, had no local government other than that provided by the parish. We have to thank Mr Francis Barnard Jennings, an Ipswich solicitor, who for some eight years worked with a few local businessmen (F B Jolly and H G Quilter were two of the prominent voices) before the

Above: **The Beach 1907** 58958

Right: **From the Beach 1899** 44513

The Central Sea Front

The Central Sea Front

Right: **The Pier 1907** 58974

The entrance to the New Pier, which was constructed between 1903 and 1905. The advertising for the entertainment reads 'The Grey Ladies', who played at the seaward end of the pier, and 'The White Coons', who performed in a tent erected to the right of this picture.

Below: **The New Shelter 1899** 44518

Another example of municipal enterprise, this shelter was adjacent to the Town Hall and provided shelter and refreshment to visitors.

The Central Sea Front

Right:
The Beach 1904 51254

This a more off-season view of the seafront area.

The Central Sea Front

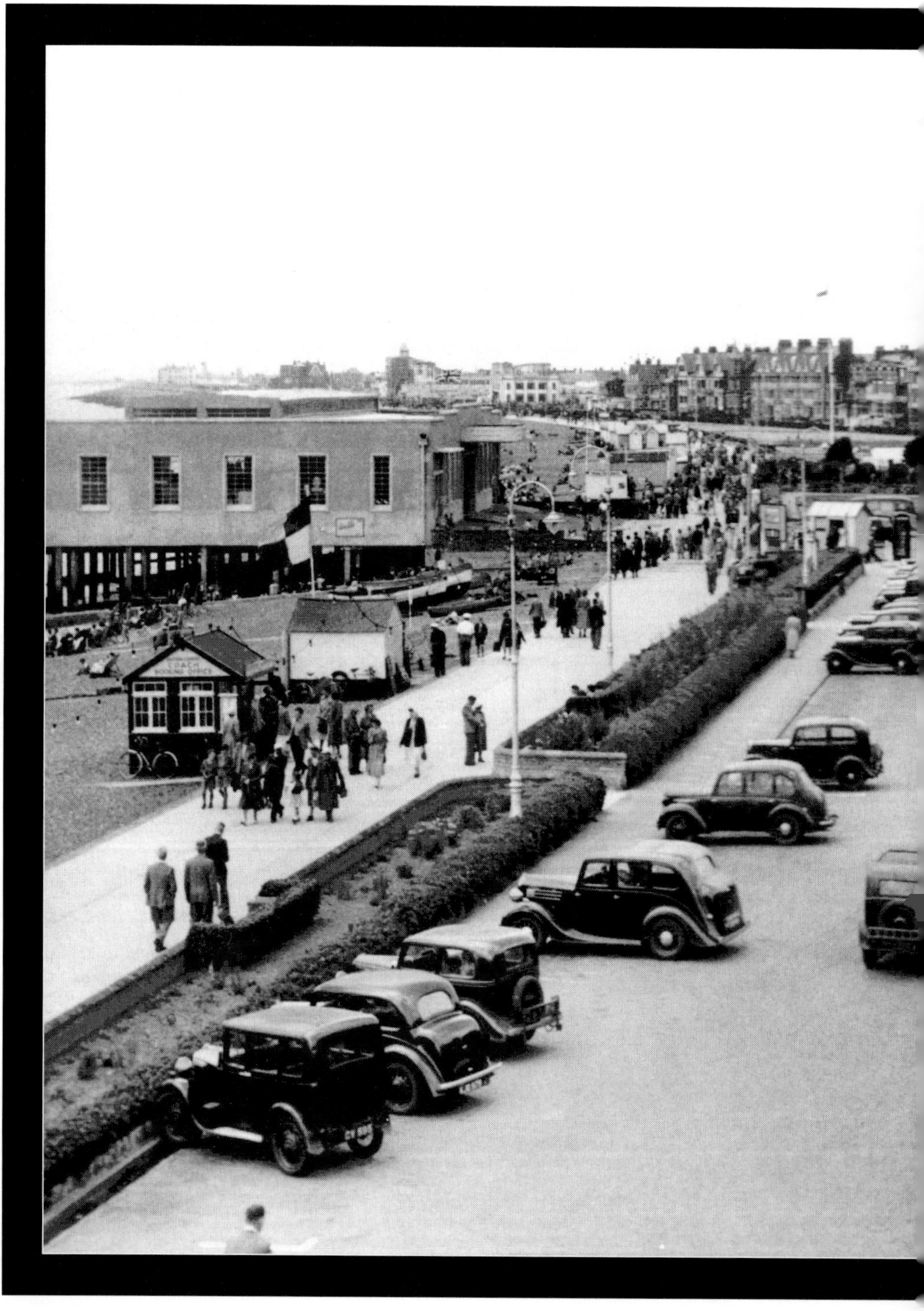

The Central Sea Front

Left: **The Pier Pavilion c1950** F16032

The Pier Pavilion was renowned for the quality of its dance floor. The Jerry Allen septet, and later quintet, played the season here for many years. The growth of motor car ownership is apparent, but parking problems are not.

Above: **The Pavilion c1955** F16050

Another view of the Pier Pavilion, with both dancing and Jerry Allen still going strong.

Below: **The Pier Bight and Pavilion c1955** F16054

The Central Sea Front

board was formed. An election was held on 29 June 1887 to appoint the twelve members; Colonel George Tomline, of dock and railway fame, easily topped the poll with 528 votes from the 571 electors, who each cast twelve votes. He then became the first Chairman of the Board, and remained so until his death in 1889.

His chairmanship did not produce the impetus for the village to develop. Tomline was an awkward, bad-tempered individual; if his view did not prevail, he would go to great lengths to see that the will of the majority was not upheld. On his death, his fellow board members were scathing about him. Shuckforth Downing, who was no hothead, said to the meeting on 4 September 1889: 'I honestly believe that Colonel Tomline was the means of keeping back the progress and improvement of Felixstowe'. The next Chairman was Felix Thornley Cobbold, whose family had been Tomline's bitter rival locally; he was the owner of the greater portion of the parish of Felixstowe.

The prime intent of the town's self-administered development as a resort was to improve the roads (58961, page 36, shows a newly-made road), which were only rough tracks. The immediate subsoil of the town is Red Crag, a mixture of dark sand and shell fragments, which blows in the wind when dry and turns to a dirty quagmire when wet. When mixed with the droppings of the growing number of horse-drawn cabs (there were 34 licensed by 1891), the Red Crag produced a surface which spoilt the fashionable ladies' dresses and shoes.

The Town Hall (44514, opposite) soon aspired to holding a Magistrates' Court, which contin-

Above: **The Zigzag 1906** 54648

Another of the sets of cliff steps, with goat carts available for hire.

Right: **Snow Hill 1906** 54646

Sets of steps were added for pedestrian access from the cliff top. The house at the top is Bulls Cliff, which was the offices for the Felixstowe & Walton Local Board until the Town Hall was built in 1892.

The Central Sea Front

Left: **West Beach 1899**
44514

The new Town Hall is in the centre of the picture, with the cab rank opposite. Note that the promenade is not built at this date.

The Central Sea Front

Right: **The Top of Bent Hill 1904** 51261

A delivery cart waits outside the shop of W Bennett, the grocer. The next building is Portman House, then comes the Waverley Hotel. The prominent building with a balcony over Stanley Road is Eastward Ho College, a boys' boarding school.

Below: **The Promenade and the Beach 1921** 71716

By 1921 the central area shows little change, as do the sun avoidance measures! A parade is in progress along the roadway.

ued until 2000. At the local government re-organisation of the 1960s, the District Council was transferred to Suffolk Coastal, who meet in Woodbridge, so the Town Hall is no longer the seat of local power. These changes have had a similar effect on our town to Tomline's antics a hundred years before. The sooner local administration and justice can be returned to the community the better!

In 54644 (page 34) the sea front gardens have now been added, together with pavement and drainage. The houses on the roadway from the far end are Swiss Cottage, Bethany, Alexandra House, the Grand Hotel, Hamilton House, Brandon House, Hale Cottage, Mount Ridley, Nos 1-3 South Beach Terrace, Nos 1-2 Sea View and Fern Villa. Most of these are still there, and so is the Pulpit Rock (in the sea, centre right). This was a trial to assess the effect of sea water on concrete. It still has sharp edges today, which speaks for its quality.

Left: **From the Pier 1906**
54637

Another off-season view, this one from the pier. The Felixstowe Swimming Club Hut has now appeared.

The Central Sea Front

The Central Sea Front

Left: **The Esplanade 1893**
32240

This is an early picture of the seafront area of Undercliff Road, before the roadway, gardens and promenade were laid. Note the position of the street lamp (right): these were installed in 1887/88.

Below Left: **The Promenade 1906** 54644

Below Centre: **South Beach Mansion 1899** 43239

Below Right: **The Promenade 1903** 50445

The influence of Douglas Tollemache is seen here. He lived in South Beach Mansion, and was responsible for building the large hotel we can now see on the cliff top (centre right). It was originally called the Balmoral, but soon became the Felix. The promenade is being constructed at this date.

Photographs 32240 and 54644 (opposite) show the houses along Undercliff. Though some are altered, the only major change is the addition of the Alexandra restaurant. Beyond this is South Beach Mansion (43239, below), built into the cliff line.

This imposing property, built for Mr Eley of Eley-Keynock cartridges, gave a very direct impetus to Felixstowe's development following 1891. In this year Princess Augusta of Schleswig-Holstein and her eldest five children (she was the wife of Kaiser William) stayed here, and at South Cottage, which is further along Hamilton Gardens, for 24 days in July and August. The visit was well publicised, and the benefits to the town as a resort were considerable.

The princess's visit put the Local Government Board in quite a spin. On the princess's arrival they allowed the street lights to remain on at all hours, and on her departure they wrote a hurried note to her, which read: 'Madam, As members of the Felixstowe and Walton local board we desire to approach your majesty, on your quitting English soil, humbly to express our hope that your majesty and your imperial children have benefited by your sojourn here and our thanks for the many proofs your majesty and your family have given of your kind thoughtfulness for the people amongst whom you have been sojourning. We wish your majesty a happy journey home'. How's that for deference! The mansion soon became the home of F J Bugg, and later Douglas Tollemache lived there (he built the Balmoral Hotel, later the Felix Hotel (51266, page 40, and 50445, right, this page).

South Beach Mansion became council offices

The Central Sea Front

The Central Sea Front

Convalescent Hill 1907 58961

We are looking west along the promenade, which is showing evidence of the much slower rate of development in this direction. Observe the road surface - all of the newly-laid roads were to this standard!

The Central Sea Front

Above: **The New Bandstand 1907** 58955

We are looking towards the New Pier. This bandstand provided an opportunity to relax. It was newly built in 1907, and seated 25 or so musicians. The canopies on the deck chairs ensure that the listeners avoid exposure to the sun.

Right: **The Promenade 1904** 51252

It is one year on from photograph 50445 (page 35): the promenade is completed, and gardens have been added between it and the roadway.

The Central Sea Front

in later life, but it has now been converted back into a private residence.

The Spa Pavilion is the next building to note in this area. It started life as a hut selling water; then a small bandstand was built here, and then a much grander bandstand appeared in 1907 (58955, opposite). No doubt the wind and the weather hampered its use, for it was incorporated into a building in 1909 which seated some 700 people. In turn this was rebuilt in 1939, but it did not survive the war intact, so it was rebuilt again in 1950. The present building, primarily used as a theatre, is being gradually updated so as to present up-to-date live entertainment - not easy in this electronic age.

I am grouping the last important buildings in this area together, as they are all are, or were, hotels: the Bath, the Felix and the Cliff. They

comprised the major part of the town's up-market accommodation for visitors. The first was the Bath Hotel (29038, opposite), which started life in 1839 as a modest establishment run by J C Cobbold. It underwent a major upgrade in 1884 after its ownership passed to H G Quilter. It was eventually burned down by suffragettes, Hilda Burkett and Florence Tunks, in April 1914. The undamaged remains now form part of the Nurses Home and Education Centre of the Bartlett Hospital.

The Felix Hotel (51266, below) was added in 1903 at the behest of D A Tollemache - his aim was to capture the upper end of the tourist market. The hotel, designed by the local architect T W Cotman, was three years in the building, and when it opened it proved successful. Brochures of the time when both the

Right: **Beach Donkeys 1891** 29038

This picture shows the Bath Hotel, which had been considerably extended in 1884. A selection of cabs await fares. The donkeys are a vital part of the holiday scene - the donkey master is Jack Rattle of Walton.

Below Right: **The Cliff Hotel 1907** 58964

The third of this trilogy of hotels is the Cliff, which appeared in 1907. It was built for the Quilter family, 'late of the Bath'. Used as a hospital during the war, it is now offices. The area where the hotel stood was known as Beacon Field, and it is believed to be the site of one of the sea beacons - hence the flagpole on the site.

Right: **The Felix Hotel 1904** 51266

The Felix Hotel added a second luxury hotel to the town. This view is from the rear of the tennis courts, with the garages on the right.

The Central Sea Front

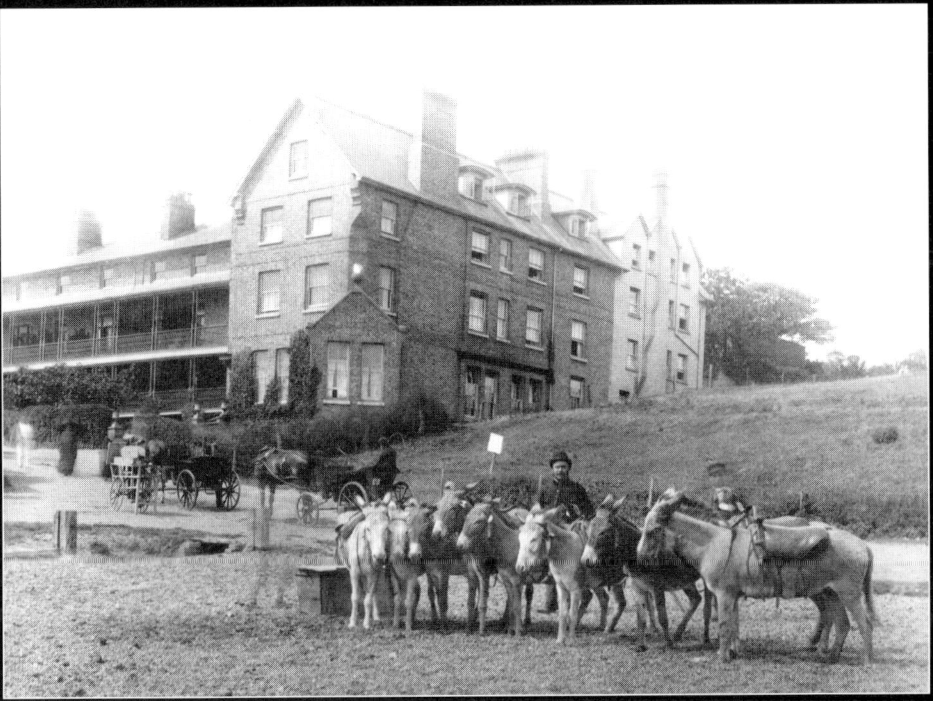

The Central Sea Front

Bath and Felix were competing for trade show that the Bath was the more expensive of the two. Ownership passed to the Great Eastern Railway in 1920. It closed as a hotel and reopened as offices for Fison's Ltd in 1952. It eventually became the apartment complex it is today.

While many hotels were built for them, the well heeled added large 'marine residences' to the town's housing stock (38678, opposite and 38683, page 44). Many of these were only used for a few weeks each year. At the time when 38678 was taken, the house on the right was a convalescent home. The row of houses in 38683 dates from the 1880s, and was known as Verandas. The view was taken from the sports ground, with the horse of Mr Borley, the groundsman, keeping the grass down. It was stabled in the Martello R Tower, now the site of the Bartlett Hospital.

As we walk along the Promenade, we can view this part of the sea front; it was added in 1903/04, the same time as the Felix Hotel was being constructed. There was a division of opinion within the town as to whether or not it was desirable to have a road running alongside the line of the Promenade. This was eventually decided by a local referendum in 1906, which voted against the road. The implications of building the Promenade and no road are probably the two most important factors influencing seafront development in Felixstowe during the 20th century.

Right:
Wolsey Gardens 1896 38678

Below Left:
Wolsey Gardens 1896 38678a

Below Right:
The Waverley Hotel 1896 38676

The Waverley is one of the hotels built around the turn of the century to cater for the seasonal demand for good class accommodation in the town.

The Central Sea Front

The Central Sea Front

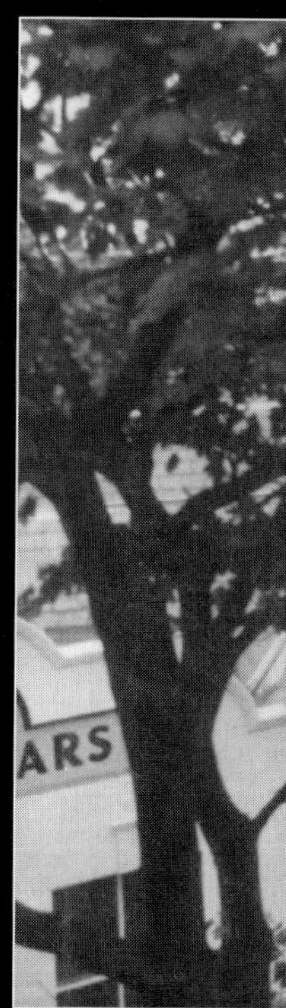

The Central Sea Front

Left: **High Beach 1896** 38683

Below Left: **The Beach 1930** 82933

By 1930 no trace of bathing machines remain, and motor-boat trips round the bay and to the Cork Lightship have taken their place. I do believe more skin is being exposed to the sun!

Below Right: **Bent Hill c1955** F16062

The old Grand Hotel on Bent Hill has now become the Grand Bars (left). The owner, Mr William Yetton-Ward, is standing on the top step. Felixstowe owes much to this gentleman's activities over many years.

North of the Sea Front

This chapter covers the area of the cliff-top northwards towards the farmland and marshes leading to the River Deben. In times past it was all farmland here; the centres of habitation were Old Felixstowe village to the east and Walton to the west (43245, page 55). It was not until the mid 19th century that any significant building took place.

John Chevallier Cobbold, the long-standing Conservative MP for Ipswich, had acquired land here. He formed the Conservative Freehold Land Society with the intention of providing homes for tradespeople in the central area together with a commercial centre. Starting in the 1850s, it proved to be a very slow-moving venture; but by the 1880s progress was apparent, with housing in Ranelagh Road, Felix Road and Cobbold Road, together with Hamilton Road's seaward end, which was called the Parade (43237, opposite) and Orwell Road (44519, page 48), which was the commercial sector.

The enterprise was renamed the Freehold Land Society, and many houses have name plaques with 'FLS' and the date of their building to this day. The venture is now the Ipswich Building Society. By 1905, Hamilton Road had extended, with shops to Cobbold Road on one side and York Road on the other (F16025, page 48). The other significant development was at the northern end of the town: in 1898 the railway was extended as far as here, and the Town Station was built. The Orwell Hotel was erected to serve the railway passengers (43240, page 49). The completion of the shopping street to the northern end of town did not follow until after the end of World War I.

The late Victorians made much of religious worship, and during the same period that commerce was flourishing, so were the churches. There was a spate of church building at this time in line with the growth of the population. The first to be built was the Evangelical Free Church in Ranelagh Road, 1871, now demolished. In Orwell Road, St John's was built in 1895 (38685, page 50). This red brick church replaced a tin chapel erected on what is now the Leisure Centre site. The impressive spire

North of the Sea Front

Above Left: **The Parade 1899**
43237

The early stage of developing Hamilton Road as the main shopping street began at this seaward end, and was called the Parade.

Below Left:
The Parade 1955 F16063

This is an interesting comparison with 43237 some 50 years later. Barclays bank (right) is still there, and the Arts Theatre (left) has survived, though it has had alternative uses - a church and a cinema are two of them.

North of the Sea Front

Left: **Bank Corner 1899** 44519

We are looking east along Orwell Road. The Methodist church was opened in 1896.

Below Left: **Hamilton Road c1950** F16025

The main street is recovering after World War II, with traders returning from exile or new ones taking their place.

Below Right: **The Orwell Hotel 1899** 43240

This newly-built hotel was erected primarily to serve the equally new town railway station, which was located opposite. The picture also gives another example of the state of the roadways at this time.

was added in 1914. Also in Orwell Road, the Methodist church was built in 1896 (44519, page 48) and the Presbyterian church in 1900 (54651, opposite). Before this, many of the non-conformist congregations had met in the Victoria Hall on Victoria Parade. St Andrew's followed in 1907 (58982, opposite). To go with this apparent piety, there were no licensed premises in Hamilton Road between the Orwell and the Grand on Bent Hill.

The Victoria Hall became the first cinema in town in 1915. It had previously been used for concerts and the like, as well as for church services on Sundays. Later it became the Arts Theatre, and is now Argos. Hamilton Road was the site of a second cinema before 1914, the Playhouse, and the Ritz in 1937. Ranelagh Gardens were established before 1900 (51260, opposite), and a theatre was built soon after; it remained a summer season attraction until the 1950s. There was always great rivalry between the Ranelagh, which was owned by the impresario Will Hammer, and the Spa, which was owned by Felixstowe Council, over the quality of their summer shows - however, both managed regularly to play to full houses.

Constable Road (58976, page 52) is an example of one of the new residential streets. Mr Chapman the provision merchant (right) moved to Granville Road the following year, 1908; Killingback's took over, and stayed there for the next 50 years. The hygiene along the street leaves much to be desired, though what is there is very good for the garden!

Above: **The Presbyterian Church 1906** 54651

St George's was built in 1900, another of the churches that were added to service the growing population.

Above: **St John's Church 1896** 38685

Right: **Ranelagh Gardens 1904** 51260

Ranelagh Gardens was added to the town's leisure attractions around 1900. It was always the rival venue for the council's summer show at the Pier and Spa Pavilions.

Above: **St Andrew's Church 1907** 58982

Yet another new church. This one lasted until 1932, when it was rebuilt in reinforced concrete.

North of the Sea Front

Constable Road 1907 58976

North of the Sea Front

North of the Sea Front

Constable's Cottage 1904 51263

This derelict building was Hornes Farmhouse, its agricultural activity ended by the residential boom. It was soon restored, and became known as Constable Cottage; this, together with nearby Constable Road (58976, page 52), give a hint of a connection with the antecedents of the painter John Constable.

North of the Sea Front

Above: **The Grove 1906** 54656

The Grove provided a shady haven for a quiet walk on a summer's day. By today's standards, the lady in the picture is decidedly overdressed.

Below: **Walton, the Village 1899** 43245

This view of Walton was taken at a time when new curbs and pavements were being laid.

Old Felixstowe

This area extends eastwards from Bath Hill in the south to Felixstowe ferry. Its origins cannot positively be identified from written sources, but there is ample evidence of Roman occupation from archaeological discoveries made in the area - a fine Samian ware globular cup of the 1st or 2nd century is now in the British Museum. It is probable that the Romans occupied a military fortification, Walton Castle. Its remains are visible at low water about 40 yards out from the shore at a spot known locally as 'The Dip'. From the Roman record, the Notitia Dignitatum, we cannot recognise Walton Castle; but as there are other definite fortification sites which similarly cannot be identified, it is reasonable to assume that the Notitia's listing is not a comprehensive one.

What is certain is that the group of buildings was destroyed on the orders of King Henry II following the abortive attempts to overthrow him in 1173 and 1176. The plots had the support of Hugh Bigod, first Earl of Norfolk, who was the leading East Anglian baron; he held the castles at Framlingham and Bungay as well as Walton. The destruction, presumably, involved the removal of the keep and its associated buildings, as there is ample evidence of the existence of the outer walls. In time, they fell into the sea as the cliff line was eroded.

There is a school of thought that suggests that the ruins of the castle were used as a church, which was founded by Saint Felix following his arrival in East Anglia in the 7th century. It may be that the place name Felixstowe derives from this event; however, there is scant evidence to support this hypothesis. Over many years, historians have regularly supported or dismissed the possibility that the legend is based on truth. At present, there seems to be a positive trend, with modern scholarship supporting the notion that the suffix 'stowe' means a very important place of religious significance, rather than the standard less assertive interpretation.

No mention is made of the castle in the Domesday survey of 1086. However, it seems likely that several Domesday vills can be iden-

Below: **Brook Lane 1906** 54653

Brook Lane is one of Felixstowe's ancient roads - it leads from the High Street to the East Beach near Cobbolds Point. The children in this charming picture have either lost their horse (or donkey) or are pulling the cart themselves.

Above: **The Golf Links 1896** 38684

Sexism ruled strongly in 1896: this is the Ladies' Clubhouse at Felixstowe Ferry Golf Club, which was founded in 1880 - the ladies' section was not formed until 1894. The fair sex also had their own 6-hole course to play on. We can also see Martello Tower T in this picture.

tified with the area forming modern Felixstowe: these are Burgh, Gulphea, Langerstuna, Oxlanda and Burgata, plus Mycelgata as a strong possible. Burgh is the most important of these settlements, and from its name it can be concluded that it includes the old castle area. There is also a reference to a church here. In total, the area valued covers some 439 acres of arable and 6.75 acres of meadow; it names 75 individuals as landholders in one form or another, and the area produced an income of £5 14s 8d to the landlords.

The remarkable figure in this survey is the 75 landholders. I stress that the Domesday survey was not, and nor did it pretend to be, a census; any interpolation of the data into population size is a dangerous practice. However, this will rarely result in an overestimate, due to the anomalies in the survey. The population size suggested by the Domesday survey was a very large one, for if the average household was as low as 5 members, the fact that there were 75 landholders mean that the population of Burgh would have been about 375. My researches confirm that this area was heavily populated in the 11th century. When I looked at the whole of the Colneis Hundred (which consists of the modern parishes of Felixstowe, Walton, Falkenham, the two Trimleys, Nacton, Levington, Bucklesham, Kirton and Hemley), the figures indicated that the population of 1086 was larger than the population recorded in the censuses taken between 1801 and 1861. This could be an indication that a considerable amount of the land was lost to the sea in the intervening centuries.

During the 14th century a manor house was built in the parish for the Bigod family. This was situated in the corner of the present town's sports ground, and it was certainly visited by King Edward III, as he confirmed charters on the borough of Ipswich from here during 1338-39. This royal visit was brought about by the king's departure from the River Deben, where his fleet assembled, to France, where he was victorious at the battle of Crecy.

The manor of Walton cum Trimley, which encompassed Felixstowe, was one of the victims in the Peasants' Revolt of 1381. A gathering of disgruntled inhabitants led by John Battisford, the rector of Bucklesham, seized the manor court rolls and burnt them, thus destroying the evidence of the services the peasants were obliged to render to the lord of the manor. These services were a source of much discontent around this time, probably due to the reduction in population as a result of the Black Death of 1349, which was particularly severe in the area.

It is still possible to walk along the route of the trackways which have been used for more than one thousand years. Some of them, particularly the Quintons Lane, Gulpher Road, Ferry Road, and Marsh Lane area, are little changed. By taking a walk, or drive, along High Road East from the Orwell Hotel to Church Road, we pass the buildings of six of the uprated farm houses (F16068, above). As recently as the 1950s, a herd of cows was

Old Felixstowe

Left: **High Road East c1955** F16068

A view of the small parade of shops in Old Felixstowe; the closest is the post office. The thatched building, left, was a public house, the Pig and Whistle, until the 1890s.

Right: **The Parish Church 1906** 54650

The parish church, dedicated to St Peter and St Paul, has early origins, but it was considerably extended in 1873. The ivy-clad tower is much lower than it would have originally been, probably to lessen its visibility from the sea.

driven from pasture on what is now the Cliff Estate to Ransomes Farm twice each day for milking. According to the detailed survey by Aaron Rathborne, in 1613 there were 51 dwellings in this area; 8 of them are described as cottages, 39 as messuage and 4 as capital messuage - these terms are indicative of the size and status of the dwelling. The reason for undertaking this survey is not known, but it seems likely that it had something to do with the church, as church lands are not included in it. The survey is very detailed, and gives a close-up look at the field patterns existing in the early 17th century.

The parish church of St Peter and St Paul (54650, page 59) is of ancient origin, probably from the 7th century. It is not uncommon for coastal churches to have large towers enabling them to be used a seamarks. In later times, however, the benefits had to be weighed against a possible enemy at sea recognising where he was by observation of landmarks such as high church towers. Certainly, this tower has been considerably reduced in height at some time. The church was much altered and also extended by the addition of transepts and a new chancel in 1873-76. In recent years it has been further extended; during these works, some of the old stonework has been uncovered, which gives some period atmosphere to the nave.

The line of large houses which extends between Bath Hill and Cobbolds Point (58959, below) is well worth seeing. Two years ago

The East Beach 1907 58959

This area of the town was where several rich families built imposing houses in the early part of the 19th century. This is another scene that is little changed today.

Felixstowe Ferry 1907 58987

most of these houses belonged to Felixstowe Ladies' College, which is no more; but their outer appearances are similar to how they looked when they were built - for the most part, they date from around 1850. The Cobbold, Fludyer, Login and Harland families were responsible for the houses, which were built for the summer residents in a style that reflected their high social status. We can see this pattern of summer-only occupation when we refer to the census schedules of 1881: census day was 31 March, so it is not surprising that at that time of the year, 71 houses out of 250 in the parish were uninhabited. Ten years later in 1891 the number of dwellings had risen to 395, with 103 being unoccupied.

Felixstowe Ferry lies to the far east of Felixstowe, at the eastward point of the peninsula at the entrance of the River Deben. The ferry carried travellers to Bawdsey on the far bank of the River Deben (58987, page 61 and 58990, page 62). The large house to the centre right of 58987 is Bawdsey Manor, which Sir Cuthbert Quilter started to build in 1886. As the transit from London was much quicker via Felixstowe, he installed a chain ferry across the river to ease the journey from the capital. It operated until 1931. The inhabitants of Felixstowe Ferry always appear to be independent of Felixstowe. Many families, such as the Newsons, the Whites, the Watts and the Clarkes, have lived here for several centuries.

Old Felixstowe

The Ferry Boat Inn 1907 58990

This inn can rank as one of the oldest sites in the town: it is mentioned in 12th-century documents, where its occupant is recorded as being in control of the entrance to the river. In 2002 the area in front of the inn was designated Millennium Green so that it might be preserved from development.

Sources

Public Record Office: Rail/390
Public Record Office: Census Returns 1841-1891, Felixstowe and Walton parishes
Suffolk Record Office: Series EF12/*/*/**
Suffolk Record Office: Series FC50/*/**

Bibliography

Felixstowe: A Pictorial History. Robert Malster (Phillimore 1992)
The Felixstowe Story. Allan Jobson (Robert Hale 1968)
Lacy's Directory. (J E Lacy 1908)
Cowells Directory 1914-1929
Kellys Directory 1950-1965
Felixstowe at Leisure. Hadwen, Smith, Twidale, White and Wylie (Privately published 1996)
The Felixstowe Railway. Quale and Bradbury (Oakwood Press 1978)
Edwardian Grand Hotel. L J Ramsey (Privately published 1995)
Old Felixstowe. Leonard Thompson (Privately published 1945)
Various unpublished items. D J Tolliday

To receive your FREE Mounted print

Cut out this voucher and return it with your remittance of £1.95 to cover postage and handling to a UK address only.* Your sepia print will be A4 in size, and mounted in a cream mount with a burgundy rule line, overall size 14 x 11 inches.

PLEASE NOTE: Many of the images used in this book are extracted from larger photographs. Those marked 'detail' or 'extract' will be isolated details from a much larger scene. The prints on offer will be of the whole image, not the detail or extract shown. Please also note that the title of your print may differ slightly from that printed in the book.

Order additional Mounted prints at HALF PRICE (only £7.49 each*)

If there are further photographs in the book you would like to order, possibly as gifts for friends and family, purchase them at half price (no additional postage and handling required).

Have your mounted prints Framed*

For an additional £14.95 per print you can have your chosen Mounted Print framed in an elegant polished wood and gilt moulding, overall size 16 x 13 inches (no additional postage and handling required).

***IMPORTANT!** This offer is only available for delivery to one address in the UK. Please forward the original voucher on this page (no copies are permitted). These special prices are only available when ordering using this voucher.

Send completed form and remittance to:

The Francis Frith Collection
Frith's Barn
Teffont
Salisbury
Wiltshire
SP3 5QP

Tel: 01722 716 376
Fax: 01722 716 881
email: sales@francisfrith.co.uk
www.francisfrith.co.uk

VOUCHER

for FREE and Reduced Price Frith Prints

Photo No/Page No	Qty	Mounted @ £7.49	Framed + £14.95	Total Cost
/	1	Free of charge*	£	£
/		£	£	£
/		£	£	£
/		£	£	£
/		£	£	£
/		£	£	£
		*Post and handling (UK only)		£1.95
		Total Order Cost		£

Book title ....

I enclose a Sterling cheque / postal order for £ ....

made payable to 'The Francis Frith Collection'

OR please debit my Mastercard / Visa / Switch / Amex card

Number ....

Issue No (Switch only) .... Valid from (Amex/Switch) ....

Expires .... Signature ....

Name Mr / Mrs / Ms ....

Address ....

....

.... Postcode ....

Daytime Tel No .... (For queries only)

Valid until 31/12/04

WHS

Free Print - see overleaf

Titles in this series

If you have enjoyed reading this book you will be pleased to know that there are 105 titles in the series - see the list below.

Look for the towns where you were born, brought up, went to school, and have lived down the years. Remember, too, that they make perfect gifts for family and friends.

Aberystwyth
Aldershot
Banbury
Barnstaple
Bedford
Beverley
Bishops Stortford
Blackburn
Braintree
Brecon
Brentwood
Bridgnorth
Bristol
Bromley
Bromsgrove
Burgess Hill
Burnley
Bury
Bury St Edmunds
Buxton *(Derbyshire)*
Camborne
Carmarthen
Caterham
Chippenham
Christchurch *(Dorset)*
Cirencester
Clacton-on-Sea
Congleton
Cowes
Crawley *(West Sussex)*
Crewe
Darlington
Devizes
Dorking
Droitwich Spa
Epsom
Farnborough *(Hampshire)*
Farnham *(Surrey)*
Felixstowe
Fleet *(Hampshire)*
Godalming
Grantham
Gravesend
Great Malvern
Great Yarmouth
Grimsby
Halifax
Harlow
Hartlepool
Haverfordwest
Henley-on-Thames
Hitchin
Hull
Huntingdon
Ilkley
Kendal
Kettering
Kidderminster
Launceston
Leamington Spa
Lewes
Llandudno
Loughborough
Lowestoft
Lytham St Annes
Macclesfield
Maldon
Margate
Market Drayton
Market Harborough
Melton Mowbray
Minehead
Newmarket *(Suffolk)*
Newton Abbot
Northampton
Ormskirk
Peterborough
Plymouth
Redcar
Rhyl
Ripon
Romsey
Ross-on-Wye
Rugby
Saffron Walden
Scunthorpe
Selby
Skegness
Skipton
St Austell
Staines
Stamford
Stevenage
Tavistock
Tenby
Torquay
Trowbridge *(Wiltshire)*
Walton-on-Thames
Weybridge
Windsor
Wisbech
Worcester
Worthing *(West Sussex)*
Yeovil
York